And the
Angels Sing

A Song Book of Classic Christmas Carols

And the
Angels Sing

A Song Book of Classic Christmas Carols

Arranged by Andrew Davis

Museum of Fine Arts, Boston

Mystical Marriage of St. Catherine (detail)
Pieter de Witte

RIZZOLI
NEW YORK

Front cover illustration:
Piero di Cosimo
Italian (Florentine), 1462–about 1521
Two Angels
Oil transferred from panel to canvas
34⅜ × 25⅜ inches
Turner Sargent Collection. 94.180

English lyrics to March of the Kings
by George W. Anthony © 1966
Theodore Presser Company.
Reprinted by permission of the publisher.

First Published in the United States of America in 1991
by RIZZOLI INTERNATIONAL PUBLICATIONS, INC.
300 Park Avenue South
New York, NY 10010 and
Museum of Fine Arts, Boston
465 Huntington Avenue
Boston, MA 02115

Library of Congress Cataloging-in-Publication Data

And the angels sing.
   1 score.
   ISBN 0-8478-1408-4
   1. Carols, English.   2. Christmas music.
M1629.3.C5A5   1991   91-17327
                                   CIP
                                    M

Project coordinators: Kathryn Sky–Peck and Susan Kvam
Designed by Christina Bliss
Music Engraved by Sonata Music Graphics, Brattleboro, VT
Special thanks to Otis Read Music, Providence, RI

ISBN 0-8478-1408-4

92 93 94 95 / 10 9 8 7 6 5 4 3 2

Printed and bound in Hong Kong

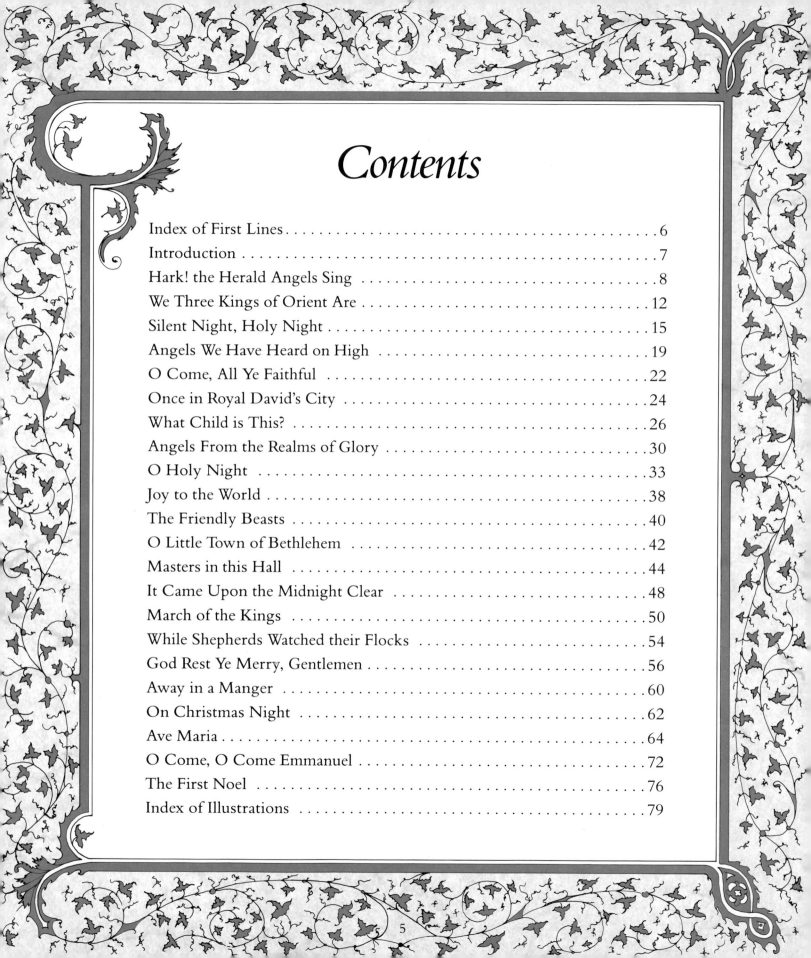

Contents

Index of First Lines

Introduction

Christmas is a time of awe and wonder, a joyous time when we celebrate the mystery of Jesus Christ's birth. The story of the miracle—the Annunciation, the journey to Bethlehem, the adoration of the shepherds, and the gifts of the Magi—has long inspired some of the world's greatest works of art. It has also inspired the music we've come to know as Christmas carols, music that has become the very embodiment of the Christmas spirit.

In this collection, we've wedded art of the Medieval and Renaissance eras—from Flanders to Florence—with the music that has endured for centuries. Among the artists represented here are such masters as Tintoretto, Botticelli, Van der Weyden, Daddi, and Schongauer—artists who gave the Christmas story humanity, mystery, and beauty, and made it accessible to us all. The classic carols we've chosen span hundreds of years, with the earliest carols dating back to the 14th century. The compositions include works by Handel, Mendelssohn, Gruber, and Schubert.

Andrew Davis has provided new arrangements specially for this edition. These arrangements are elegant yet simple to play, and retain the beauty and familiarity of the traditional versions. The music has been arranged for piano with accompaniments for any C instrument, such as recorder, flute, or violin. The arrangements also include chords suitable for instruments such as guitar, autoharp, or mandolin.

We hope this collection becomes a traditional part of the Christmas magic in your home. And as you turn the pages, listen: can you hear the angels singing? All that's missing is your voice raised in song!

Hark! The Herald Angels Sing

Two Angels, Piero di Cosimo

Words: adapted from a hymn by Charles Wesley
Music: adapted from a chorus by Felix Mendelssohn

Andante con moto

Hark! the her - ald an - gels sing, —

Glo - ry to the new - born King!

Peace on earth and mer - cy mild, — God and sin - ners rec - on - ciled.

Joy - ful all ye na - tions rise, — Join the tri - umph of the skies, —

(Please turn the page)

With th'an- gel- ic host pro- claim, Christ is— born in Beth- le- hem!

Hark! the her- ald an- gels sing, Glo- ry— to the new-born King.

2. Christ, by highest heav'n adored;
    Christ, the everlasting Lord;
    Late in time behold Him come,
    Offspring of the Virgin's womb.
        Veil'd in flesh the Godhead see;
        Hail th'Incarnate Deity,
        Pleased as Man with man to dwell,
        Jesus, our Emmanuel! (chorus)

3. Mild He lays His glory by,
    Born that man no more may die,
    Born to raise the sons of earth,
    Born to give them second birth.
        Ris'n with healing in His wings,
        Light and life to all He brings,
        Hail, the Sun of Righteousness!
        Hail, the heav'n born Prince of Peace! (chorus)

Adoration of the Magi, Workshop of Bartholome Zeitblom

We Three Kings Of Orient Are

Words: John H. Hopkins

Music: John H. Hopkins

Joyously

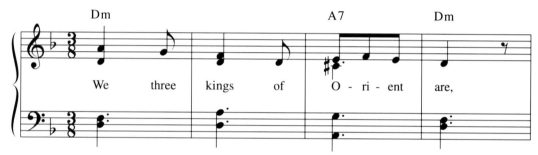

We three kings of O - ri - ent are,

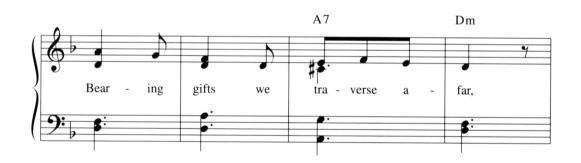

Bear - ing gifts we tra - verse a - far,

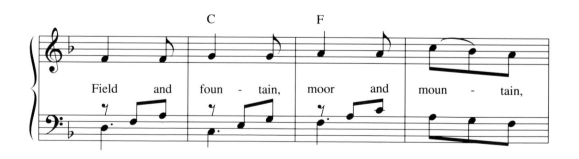

Field and foun - tain, moor and moun - tain,

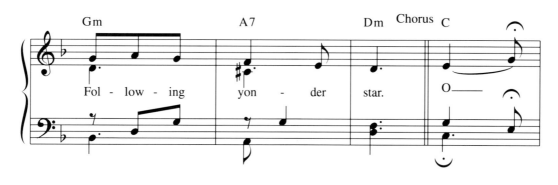

| Gm | A7 | Dm Chorus | C |

Fol - low - ing yon - der star. O—

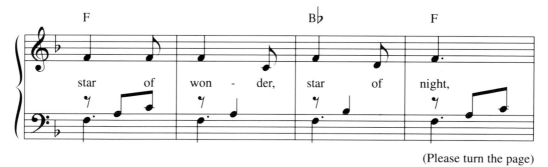

| F | B♭ | F |

star of won - der, star of night,

(Please turn the page)

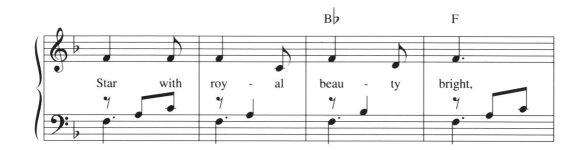

Star with roy - al beau - ty bright,

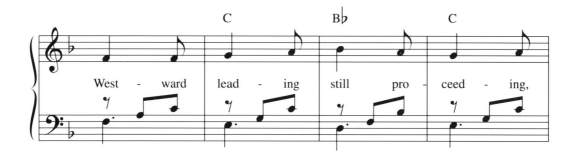

West - ward lead - ing still pro - ceed - ing,

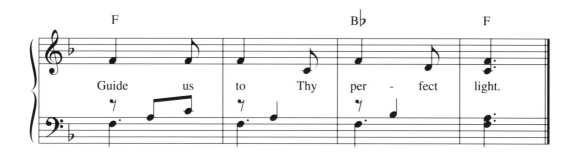

Guide us to Thy per - fect light.

2. Born a King on Bethlehem's plain,
   Gold I bring to crown Him again,
   King forever, ceasing never,
   Over us all to reign. (chorus)

3. Frankincense to offer have I,
   Incense owns a Deity nigh.
   Prayer and praising, all men raising,
   Worship Him, God most high. (chorus)

4. Myrrh is mine, its bitter perfume
   Breathes a life of gathering gloom;
   Sorrowing, sighing, bleeding, dying,
   Sealed in the stone cold tomb. (chorus)

5. Glorious now behold Him arise,
   King and God and sacrifice.
   Alleluia, Alleluia,
   Earth to heav'n replies. (chorus)

Silent Night, Holy Night

Words: Joseph Mohr

Music: Franz Gruber

Serenely

Si - lent night, ho - ly night,

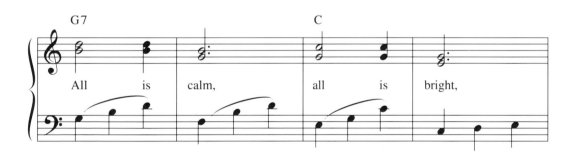

All is calm, all is bright,

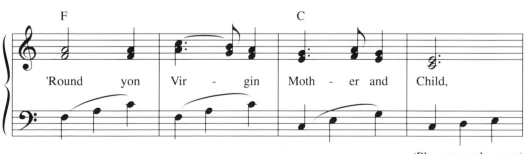

'Round yon Vir - gin Moth - er and Child,

(Please turn the page)

Madonna and Child, Luis de Morales

Ho - ly in - fant so ten - der and mild,

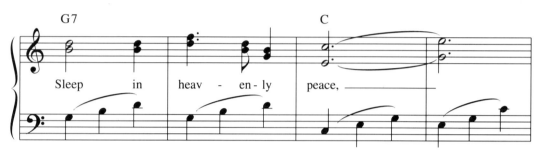

Sleep in heav - en - ly peace, _____

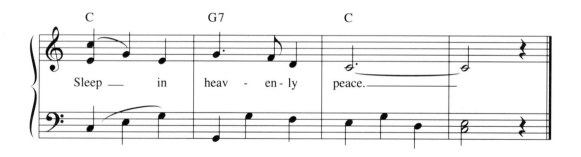

Sleep ___ in heav - en - ly peace. _____

2. Silent night, holy night,
   Shepherds quake at the sight.
   Glories stream from heaven afar,
   Heav'nly hosts sing Alleluia.
   Christ the Saviour is born!
   Christ the Saviour is born!

3. Silent night, holy night,
   Son of God, love's pure light.
   Radiant beams from Thy holy face,
   With the dawn of redeeming grace,
   Jesus, Lord, at Thy birth,
   Jesus, Lord, at Thy birth.

Archangel Gabriel
Master of the Miraculous Annunciation of Ss. Annunziata
18

Angels We Have Heard On High

Scenes from the Life of Saint John the Baptist (detail)
Master of Saint Severin

Music: traditional French

Joyously

An-gels we have heard on high, Sweet-ly sing-ing o'er the plains,

And the moun-tains in re-ply, Ech-o-ing their joy-ous strains:

(Please turn the page)

2. Shepherds, why this jubilee?
   Why your joyous strains prolong?
   What the gladsome tidings be,
   Which inspire your heavenly song? (chorus)

3. Come to Bethlehem and see
   Him whose birth the angels sing.
   Come adore on bended knee
   Christ the Lord, the newborn King. (chorus)

4. See Him in a manger laid
   Whom the angels praise above.
   Mary, Joseph, lend your aid,
   While we raise our hearts in love. (chorus)

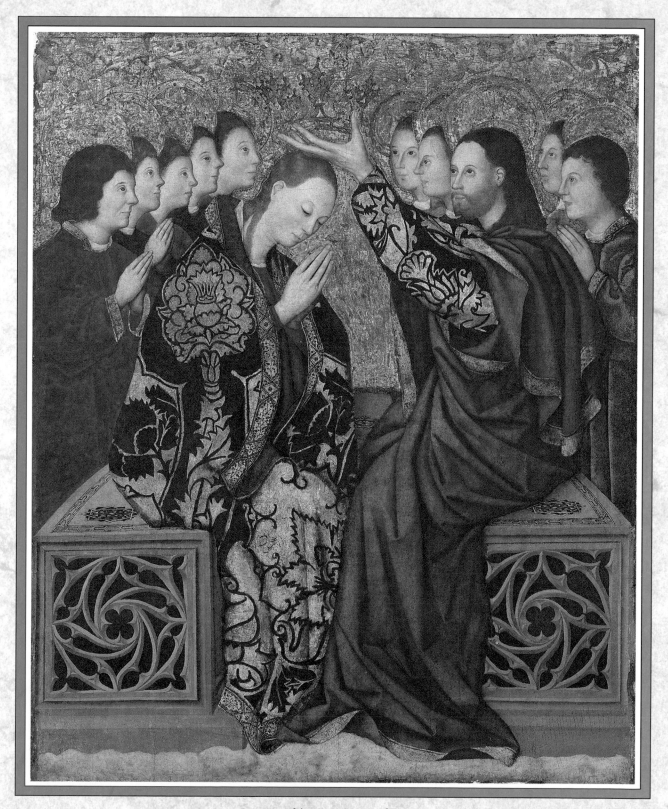

Coronation of the Virgin, Master of Bonastre

O Come, All Ye Faithful

Words: J.F. Wade, translated by Frederick Oakley
Music: J.F. Wade

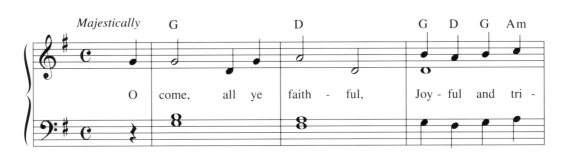

O come, all ye faith - ful, Joy - ful and tri -

um - phant, O come ye, O come— ye, to Beth - le -

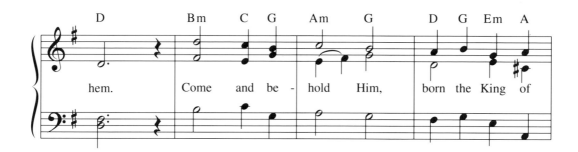

hem. Come and be-hold Him, born the King of

Chorus

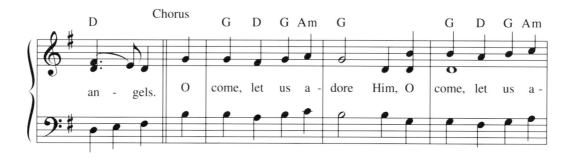

an - gels. O come, let us a - dore Him, O come, let us a -

dore Him, O come, let us a - dore Him,— Christ—— the Lord.

2. Adeste fideles,
    Laeti triumphantes,
    Venite, venite in Bethlehem.
    Natum videte, regem angelorum.
        Venite adoremus,
        Venite adoremus,
        Venite adoremus, Dominum.

3. Sing, choirs of angels,
    Sing in exultation,
    Sing, all ye citizens of heav'n above:
    Glory to God in the highest. (chorus)

4. Yea, Lord, we greet Thee,
    Born this happy morning;
    Jesus, to Thee be glory giv'n.
    Word of the Father, now in flesh appearing. (chorus)

Once In
Royal David's City

Virgin and Child Enthroned with Angels, Neri di Bicci

Words: Cecil F. Alexander

Music: Henry J. Gauntlett

Moderato

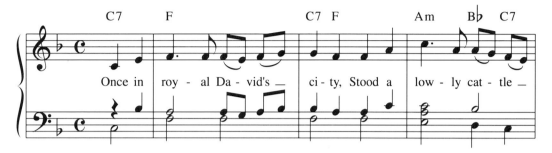

Once in roy - al Da - vid's __ ci - ty, Stood a low - ly cat - tle __

shed; Where a moth- er laid — her __ ba - by, In a man - ger for — His __

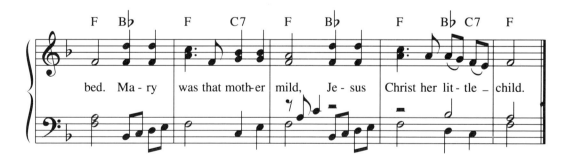

bed. Ma - ry was that moth-er mild, Je - sus Christ her lit - tle _ child.

2. He came down to earth from heaven,
Who is God and Lord of all,
And His shelter was a stable,
And His cradle was a stall;
With the poor, and mean, and lowly,
Lived on earth our Saviour holy.

3. And at last our eyes shall see Him,
Through His own redeeming love;
For that child so dear and gentle
Is our Lord in heav'n above;
And He leads His children on
To the place where He is gone.

What Child Is This?

Words: William Chatterton Dix

Music: traditional English

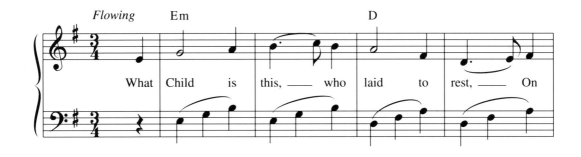

What Child is this, who laid to rest, On

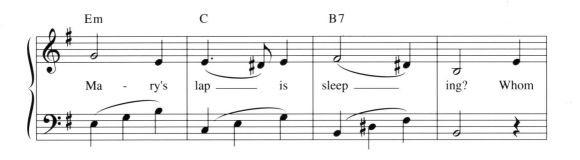

Ma - ry's lap is sleep ing? Whom

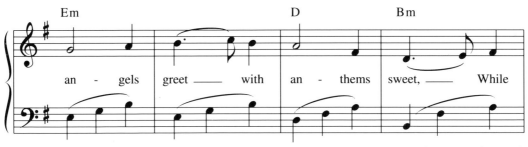

an - gels greet with an - thems sweet, While

(Please turn the page)

Virgin and Child, Bramantino

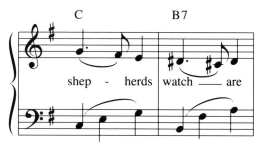

shep - herds watch ⎯ are

keep - ing?

Chorus

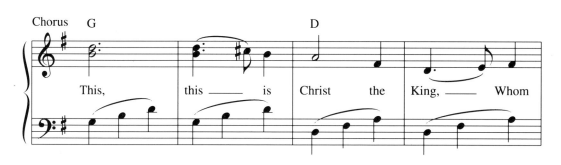

This, this ⎯ is Christ the King, ⎯ Whom

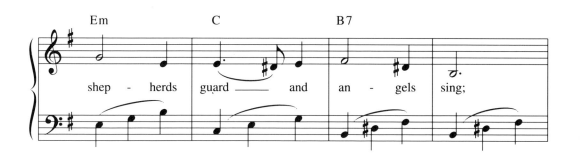

shep - herds guard ⎯ and an - gels sing;

28

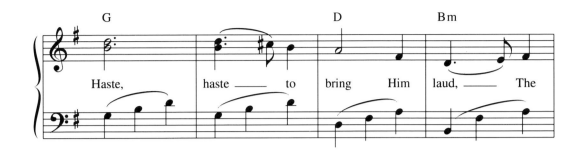

Haste, haste ——— to bring Him laud, ——— The

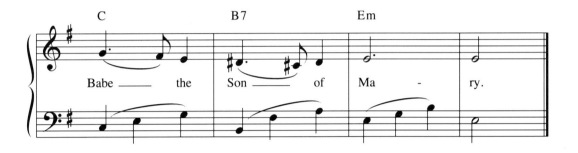

Babe ——— the Son ——— of Ma - ry.

2. Why lies He in such mean estate
   Where ox and ass are feeding?
   Good Christian, fear for sinners here
   The silent Word is pleading. (chorus)

3. So bring Him incense, gold and myrrh,
   Come, peasant, king, to own Him,
   The King of kings salvation brings,
   Let loving hearts enthrone Him. (chorus)

Angels From The Realms Of Glory

Jeremiah with Two Angels (detail), Gherardo Starnina

Words: James Montgomery
Music: Henry Smart

With spirit

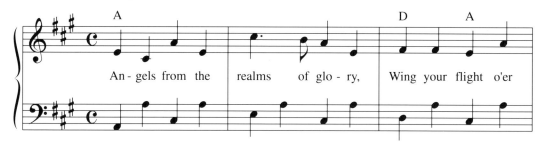

An - gels from the realms of glo - ry, Wing your flight o'er

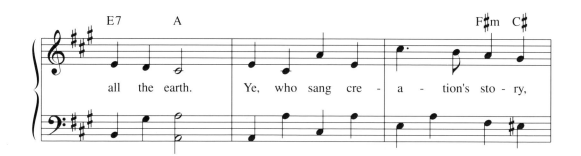

all the earth. Ye, who sang cre - a - tion's sto - ry,

Now pro - claim Mes - si - ah's birth. Come and wor - ship!

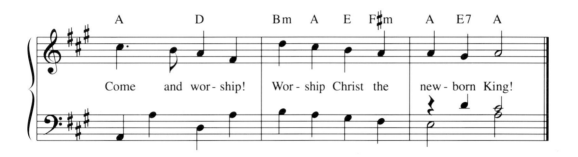

Come and wor - ship! Wor - ship Christ the new - born King!

2. Shepherds in the field abiding,
   Watching o'er your flocks by night.
   God with man is now residing,
   Yonder shines the infant Light. (chorus)

3. Sages, leave your contemplations,
   Brighter visions beam afar.
   Seek the great Desire of nations;
   Ye have seen his natal star. (chorus)

Angel of the Annunciation, Martin Schongauer

O Holy Night

Words: translated from French by John S. Dwight

Music: Adolph Adam

Andante

O Ho - ly night!_____ the stars are bright - ly

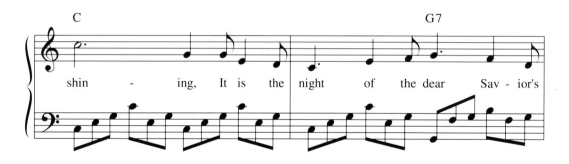

shin - ing, It is the night of the dear Sav - ior's

birth._____ Long lay the

(Please turn the page)

Fall———————— on your knees,——————— Oh,

hear———————— the an - gel voi - ces! O

(Please turn the page)

Jeremiah with Two Angels , Gherardo Starnina

Virgin and Child with the Young Saint John the Baptist
Workshop of Botticelli

37

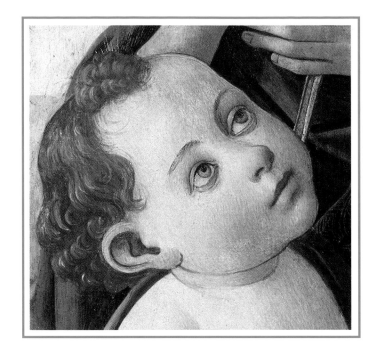

Joy To The World

Words: Isaac Watts
Music: anonymous.

Allegretto

Joy to the world! the Lord is come! Let

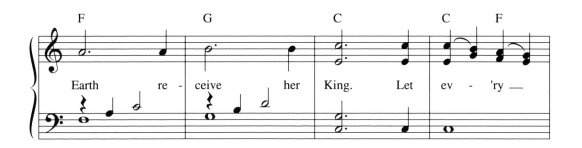

Earth re - ceive her King. Let ev - 'ry —

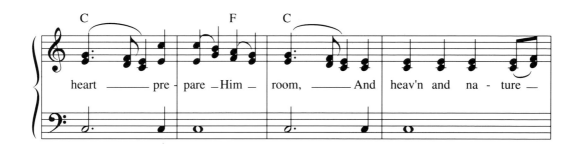

heart ——— pre –pare –Him – room, ——— And heav'n and na - ture —

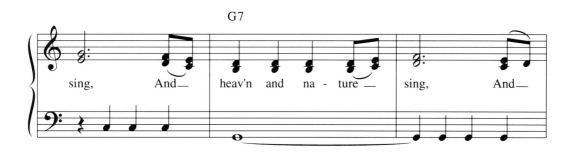

sing, And— heav'n and na - ture — sing, And—

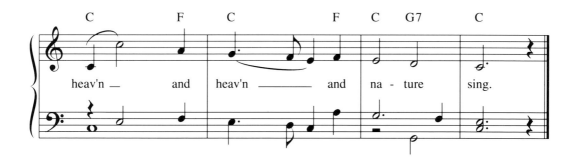

heav'n — and heav'n ——— and na - ture sing.

2. Joy to the World! the Saviour reigns.
   Let men their songs employ,
   While fields and floods, rocks, hills and plains,
   Repeat the sounding joy.

3. He rules the world with truth and grace,
   And makes the nations prove
   The glories of His righteousness,
   And wonders of His love.

The Friendly Beasts

Nativity, Martin Schongauer

Words: Robert Davis
Music: traditional French

Moderato

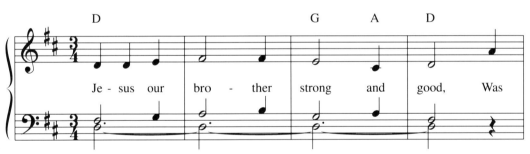

Je - sus our bro - ther strong and good, Was

hum - bly born in a sta - ble rude. The

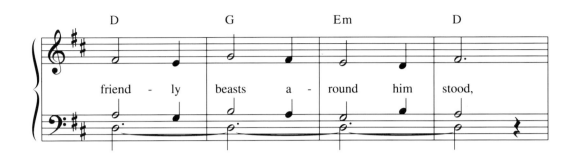

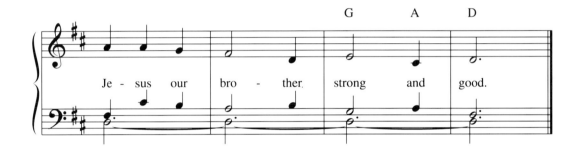

2.	"I," said the donkey, shaggy and brown,
	"I carried His mother uphill and down;
	I carried her safely to Bethlehem town."
	"I" said the donkey, shaggy and brown.

3.	"I," said the cow, all white and red,
	"I gave Him my manger for a bed;
	I gave Him my hay to pillow His head."
	"I," said the cow, all white and red.

4.	"I," said the sheep with curly horn,
	"I gave Him wool for His blanket warm;
	He wore my coat on Christmas morn."
	"I," said the sheep with curly horn.

5.	"I," said the camel, yellow and black,
	"Over the desert upon my back;
	I brought Him gifts in the wise men's pack."
	"I," said the camel, yellow and black.

6.	"I," said the dove from the rafters high,
	"I cooed Him to sleep that He should not cry;
	We cooed Him to sleep, my mate and I."
	"I," said the dove from the rafters high.

7.	Thus every beast by some good spell,
	In the stable dark was glad to tell
	Of the gift they gave Emmanuel,
	The gift they gave Emmanuel.

O Little Town Of Bethlehem

Words: Phillips Brooks
Music: Lewis H. Redner

Virgin of Humility (detail), Giovanni di Paolo di Grazia

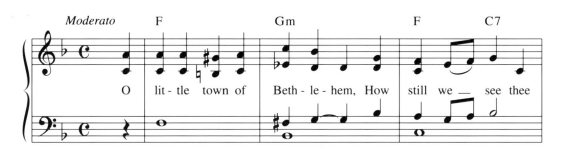

O lit - tle town of Beth - le - hem, How still we — see thee

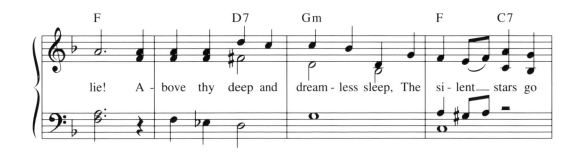

lie! A - bove thy deep and dream - less sleep, The si - lent — stars go

by.   Yet   in thy dark streets   shin - eth The   ev - er - last - ing

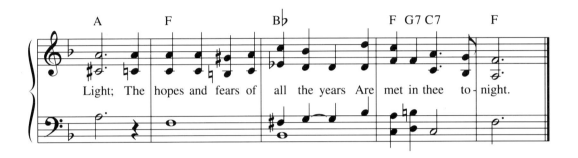

Light; The hopes and fears of   all the years Are met in thee   to - night.

2. For Christ is born of Mary,
   And gathered all above,
   While mortals sleep, the angels keep
   Their watch of wond'ring love.
     O morning stars, together
     Proclaim the holy birth!
     And praises sing to God the King,
     And peace to men on earth.

3. How silently, how silently,
   The wondrous gift is giv'n!
   So God imparts to human hearts
   The blessings of His heav'n.
     No ear may hear His coming,
     But in this world of sin,
     Where meek souls will receive Him, still
     The dear Christ enters in.

4. O holy child of Bethlehem!
   Descend to us we pray.
   Cast out our sin and enter in,
   Be born in us today.
     We hear the Christmas angels
     The great glad tidings tell;
     O come to us, abide with us,
     Our Lord Emmanuel!

Masters In This Hall

Saint Luke Painting the Virgin, Rogier van der Weyden

Words: William Morris
Music: traditional French

Vigorously

Cm

Mas - ters in this

G7

hall, _____

Cm   G7   Cm   G7

Hear ye news to - day, _____ Brought from o - ver seas, And

simile

Chorus

Cm   G7   Cm   Cm   G7   Cm

ev - er I you pray:_____   Now-ell! Now-ell! Now - ell!
                             Now-ell! Now-ell! Now - ell!

(Please turn the page)

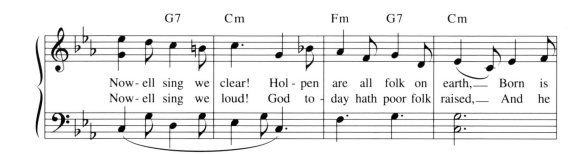

Now-ell sing we clear! Hol - pen are all folk on earth,— Born is
Now-ell sing we loud! God to - day hath poor folk raised,— And he

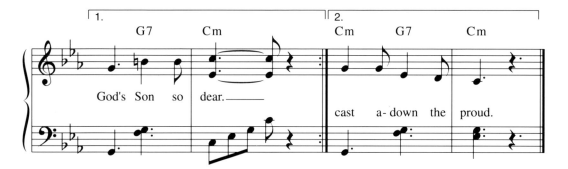

1.
God's Son so dear.———

2.
cast a- down the proud.

2. Then to Bethl'em town
   Went we two by two,
   In a sorry place
   We heard the oxen low. (chorus)

3. Ox and ass Him know
   Kneeling on their knee,
   Wondrous joy had I
   This little babe to see. (chorus)

4. This is Christ, the Lord,
   Master be ye glad!
   Christmas is come in
   And no folk should be sad! (chorus)

*Virgin and Child with Saints Jerome and Anthony of Padua
and Two Angels,* Francesco di Giorgio

47

It Came Upon The Midnight Clear

Words: Edmund H. Sears

Music: Richard S. Willis

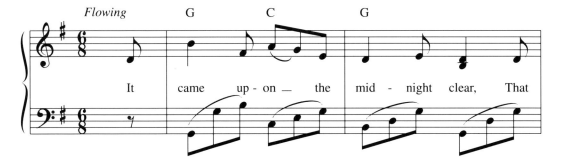

It came up-on — the mid - night clear, That

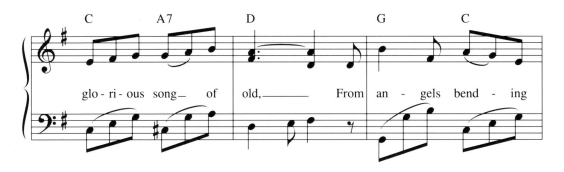

glo - ri - ous song — of old, From an - gels bend - ing

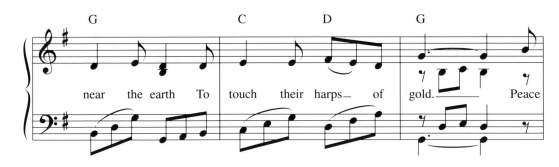

near the earth To touch their harps — of gold. Peace

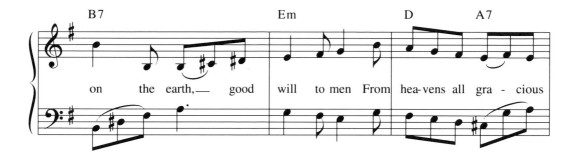

on the earth,— good will to men From hea-vens all gra - cious

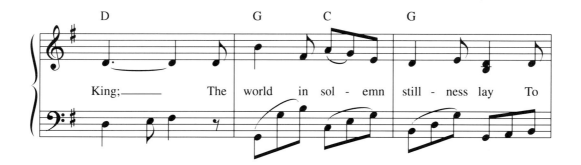

King;—— The world in sol - emn still - ness lay To

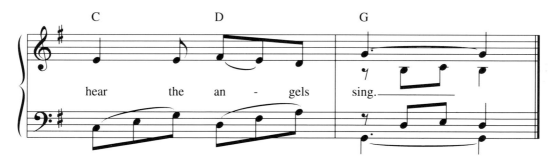

hear the an - gels sing.——

2. Still through the cloven skies they come
   With peaceful wings unfurled,
   And still their heav'nly music floats
   O'er all the weary world.
   Above its sad and lowly plains
   They bend on hov'ring wing,
   And ever o'er its Babel-sounds
   The blessed angels sing.

3. O ye, beneath life's crushing load,
   Whose forms are bending low,
   Who toil along the climbing way
   With painful steps and slow,
   Look now! for glad and golden hours
   Come swiftly on the wing;
   O rest beside the weary road
   And hear the angels sing!

March Of The Kings

Words: translated from French by George Anthony   Music: anonymous, 13th c.

Steadily

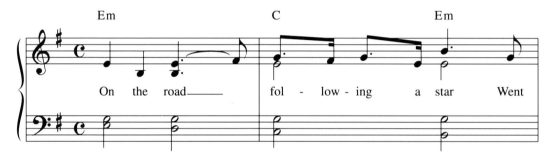

On the road____ fol - low - ing a star Went

three great Kings___ who had trav - eled far;___ Their___

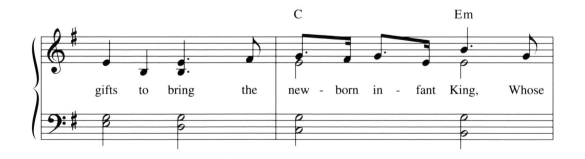

gifts to bring the new - born in - fant King, Whose

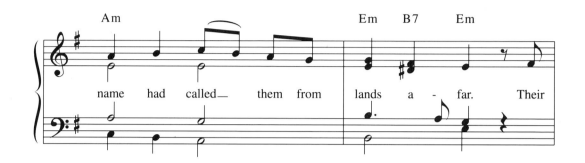

name had called— them from lands a - far. Their

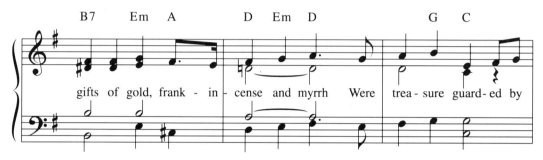

gifts of gold, frank - in - cense and myrrh Were trea - sure guard - ed by

(Please turn the page)

Adoration of the Magi, Tintoretto

Symbol of St. Matthew, Martin Schongauer

Flight into Egypt, Master of the Schretlen Circumcision

While Shepherds Watched Their Flocks By Night

Words: Nahum Tate (from the Gospel of St. Luke)

Music: G. F. Handel

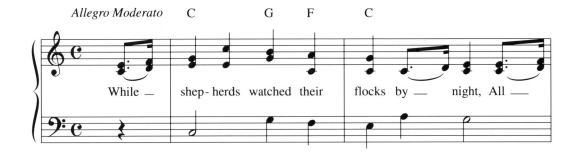

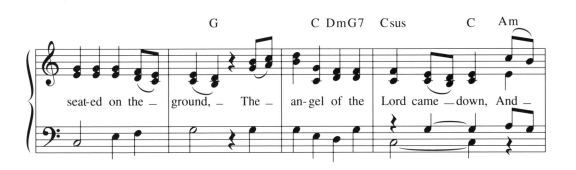

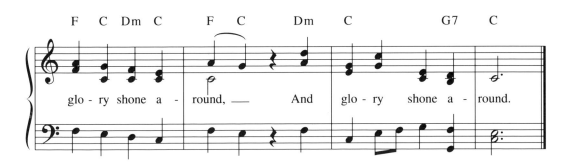

2. "Fear not," said he, for mighty dread
   Had seized their troubled mind;
   "Glad tidings of great joy I bring
   To you and all mankind."

3. "To you in David's town, this day
   Is born of David's line
   The Saviour who is Christ the Lord,
   And this shall be the sign:"

4. "The heav'nly Babe you there shall find
   To human view displayed,
   All meanly wrapped in swathing bands,
   And in a manger laid."

5. Thus spake the seraph, and forthwith
   Appeared a shining throng
   Of angels praising God, who thus
   Addressed their joyful song:

6. "All glory be to God on high
   And to the earth be peace;
   Good will henceforth from heav'n to men
   Begin and never cease."

God Rest Ye Merry Gentlemen

Saint Matthias and Saint Matthew
Master of the Holy Kinship

Words: traditional English   Music: 18th c. English

(Please turn the page)

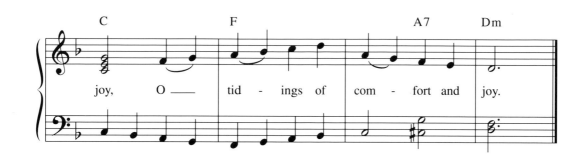

C   F   A7   Dm

joy,   O —— tid - ings of   com - fort and   joy.

2. From God our heavenly Father
   A blessed angel came;
   And unto certain shepherds
   Brought tidings of the same;
   How that in Bethlehem was born
   The Son of God by name. (chorus)

3. "Fear not, then" said the angel,
   "Let nothing you affright;
   This day is born a Saviour
   Of a pure virgin bright,
   To free all those who trust in Him
   From Satan's power and might." (chorus)

4. Now to the Lord sing praises,
   All you within this place,
   And with true love and brotherhood
   Each other now embrace;
   This holy tide of Christmas
   Doth bring redeeming grace. (chorus)

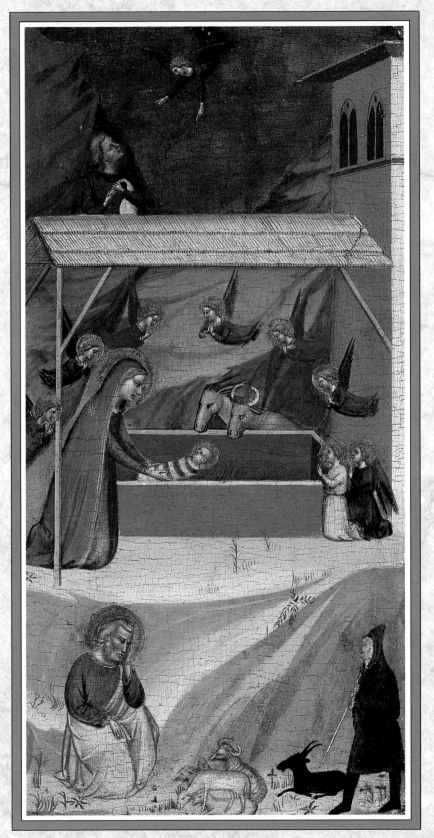

Nativity, Bernardo Daddi

59

Away In A Manger

Words: traditional American
Music: traditional American

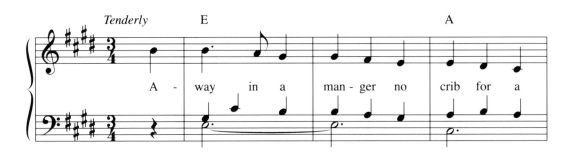

Tenderly

A - way in a man - ger no crib for a

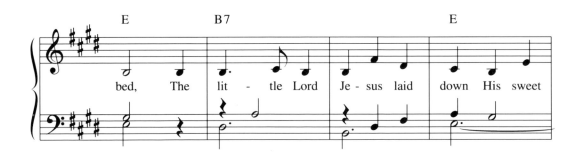

bed, The lit - tle Lord Je - sus laid down His sweet

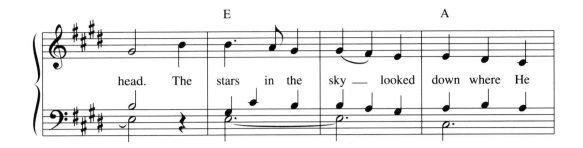

head. The stars in the sky — looked down where He

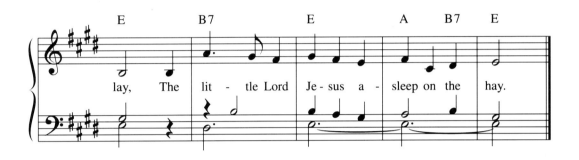

lay, The lit - tle Lord Je - sus a - sleep on the hay.

2. The cattle are lowing, the Baby awakes,
   But little Lord Jesus no crying He makes.
   I love Thee, Lord Jesus, look down from the sky,
   And stay by my cradle till morning is nigh.

3. Be near me, Lord Jesus, I ask Thee to stay
   Close by me forever, and love me, I pray.
   Bless all the dear children in Thy tender care,
   And take us to heaven to live with Thee there.

On Christmas Night

Words: traditional English
Music: traditional English

Virgin and Child, Master of the Saint Barbara Altar

On Christ - mas night all Christ - ians sing, To

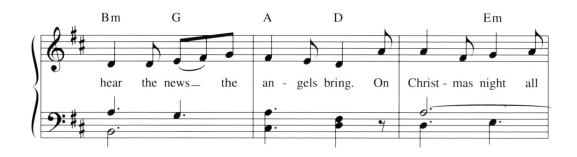

hear the news— the an - gels bring. On Christ - mas night all

Christ - ians sing, To hear the news— the an - gels bring.

News of great joy,— news of— great mirth,

News of our mer - ci - ful— King's birth

2. Then why should men on earth be so sad,
    Since our Redeemer made us glad;
    When from our sin He set us free,
    All for to gain our liberty?

3. When sin departs before His grace,
    Then life and health come in its place.
    Angels and men with joy may sing,
    All for to see the newborn King.

4. All out of darkness we have light,
    Which made the angels sing this night:
    "Glory to God and peace to men,
    Now and for evermore. Amen."

Ave Maria

Virgin and Child, Lippo Memmi

Words: translated from Latin by Sir Walter Scott
Music: Franz Schubert

Largo

(Please turn the page)

(Please turn the page)

(Please turn the page)

Virgin Adoring the Child, Sebastiano di Bartolo Mainardi

The Three Genii, Albrecht Dürer

O Come,
O Come
Emmanuel

The Annunciation (detail), Giuliano di Simone

Words: translated from the
Latin by John M. Neale
Music: 13th c. French plainsong

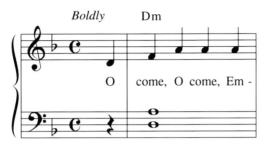

Boldly

O come, O come, Em -

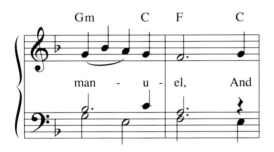

man - u - el, And

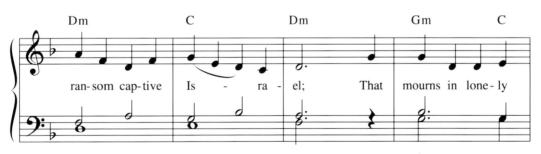

ran-som cap-tive Is - ra - el; That mourns in lone - ly

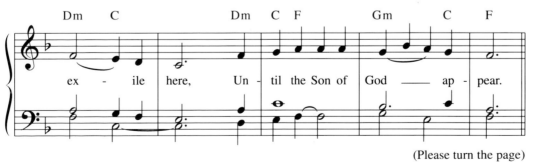

ex - ile here, Un - til the Son of God ____ ap - pear.

(Please turn the page)

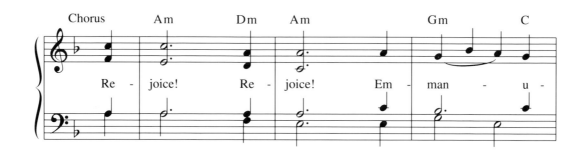

Re - joice! Re - joice! Em - man - u -

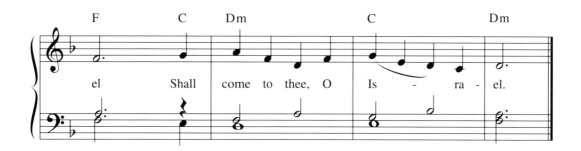

el Shall come to thee, O Is - ra - el.

2. O come, Thou Dayspring, come and cheer
   Our spirits by Thine advent here;
   Disperse the gloomy clouds of night,
   And death's dark shadows put to flight (Chorus)

3. O come, Thou Key of David, come,
   And open wide our heav'nly home.
   Make safe the way that leads on high,
   And close the path to misery. (Chorus)

Assumption of the Virgin
Niccolo di Ser Sozzo Tegliacci and Workshop

The First Noel

Words: traditional English   Music: traditional English

Moderato

The — first —— No - el the — an - gel did

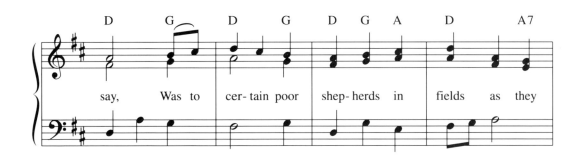

say, Was to cer- tain poor shep- herds in fields as they

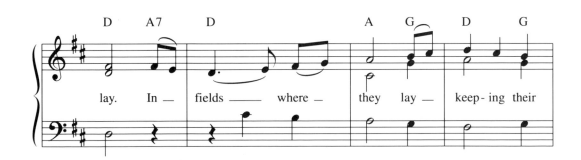

lay. In — fields —— where — they lay — keep- ing their

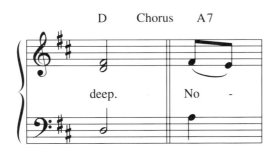

(Please turn the page)

The Archangel Michael, "Peregrinus"

2. They look-ed up and saw a star
   Shining in the east beyond them far,
   And to the earth it gave great light,
   And so it continued both day and night.
   (chorus)

3. And by the light of that same star
   Three wise men came from country far;
   To seek for a king was their intent,
   And to follow the star wherever it went.
   (chorus)

4. This star drew nigh to the northwest,
   O'er Bethlehem it took its rest,
   And there it did both stop and stay
   Right over the place where Jesus lay.
   (chorus)

5. Then entered in those wise men three
   Full rev'rently upon their knee,
   And offered there in His presence
   Their gold, and myrrh, and frankincense.
   (chorus)

6. Then let us all with one accord
   Sing praises to our heav'nly Lord;
   That hath made heav'n and earth of naught,
   And with His blood mankind hath bought.
   (chorus)

Index

Memmi, Lippo
(Filippo di Memmo, called Lippo Memmi)
Italian (Sienese), active 1317–1347
Virgin and Child
Tempera on panel, 29¾ × 21⅞ inches
Charles Potter Kling Fund
36.144

Luis de Morales
Spanish, about 1509–1586
Madonna and Child
Oil on panel, 18⅛ × 13⅝ inches
Gift of Misses Aimée and Rosamond Lamb
1978.680

Giovanni di Paolo di Grazia
Italian (Sienese), active about 1420–died 1482
The Virgin of Humility (detail)
Tempera on panel, 21⅞ × 16⅝ inches
Maria Antoinette Evans Fund
30.772

"Peregrinus"
(presumably Pellegrino di Giovanni di Antonio)
Attributed to Italian (Perugian), active 1428
The Archangel Michael
Tempera on panel, 39⅜ × 14⅝ inches
Charles Potter Kling Fund
68.22

Schongauer, Martin
German, before 1440–91
Angel of the Annunciation
Engraving
Gift of Mrs. Lydia Evans Tunnard
63.2876

The Nativity
Stephen Bullard Fund
19.1453

Symbol of St. Matthew
Engraving, 3⅝ x 3⅝ inches round
Horatio Greenough Curtis Fund
44.606

Guiliano di Simone
Italian (Lucchese) active 4th quarter, 14th century
The Annunciation, detail from *The Crucifixion
with the Virgin, Saints John and
Mary Magdalen and Two Donors,
and the Annunciation*
Tempera on panel,
32⅜ × 18¾ inches overall;
design area 27 × 14⅜ inches
Seth K. Sweetzer Fund
22.403

Starnina, Gherardo
Italian (Florentine), 1354–1409/13
Jeremiah with Two Angels (detail)
Tempera on panel
Gift of Mrs. Thomas O. Richardson
20.1857

Niccolò di Ser Sozzo Tegliacci and Workshop
Italian (Sienese), active 1334–1363
Assumption of the Virgin
Detail from *The Death and Assumption
of the Virgin with Saints Augustine,
Peter and John the Evangelist and a
Deacon Saint; and Christ Blessing with David,
Saint John the Evangelist, Solomon
and Ezekial*
Tempera on panel. Overall: 104⅜ × 84½ inches
Center panel, from which detail is taken
78 × 34⅜ inches
Gift of Martin Brimmer
83.175b

Tintoretto, Domenico
(Domenico Robusti, called Domenico Tintoretto)
Italian (Venetian), 1560–1635
Adoration of the Magi
Oil on canvas, 57⅞ × 116⅛ inches
Hebert James Pratt Fund
26.142

Rogier van der Weyden
Flemish, about 1400–1464
Saint Luke Painting the Virgin and Child
Oil and tempera on panel
53⅛ × 42⅝ inches
Gift of Mr. and Mrs. Henry Lee Higginson
93.153

Pieter de Witte (called Pietro Candido)
Flemish (worked in Florence and Munich)
about 1548–1628
The Mystical Marriage of St. Catherine (detail)
Oil on canvas, 89 × 62⅝ inches
Henry H. and Zoë Oliver Sherman Fund
1980.72

Zeitblom, Bartholome, Workshop of
German, 1455/60–1518/22
Adoration of the Magi
Oil on panel with fabric ground
62⅜ × 40⅞ inches
Gift of Mr. and Mrs. Frederick Starr
50.2720